DECORATING WITH CARPETS

A FINE FOUNDATION

DECORATING WITH CARPETS

A FINE FOUNDATION

ASHLEY STARK KENNER AND **CHAD STARK**

WITH Heather Smith MacIsaac

■ ■ ■

THE VENDOME PRESS ■ NEW YORK

CONTENTS

INTRODUCTION

Our fathers have shared an office in Stark's New York showroom for almost half a century. To us, they simply know everything about carpet. Beyond their own chapter and verse gleaned from years in the family business, dozens of books about carpet fill the shelves in their office. There are books on design like Owen Jones's *Grammar of Ornament*, from which our grandfather, who founded Stark Carpet, pulled inspiration for geometric carpets. His notations throughout the book always bring him and his enthusiasm for carpets back to life for us.

There are books about the history of carpet, the making of carpet, specific kinds of carpet, and the care and repair of carpet. It's the most comprehensive library on the subject of carpets that we've ever encountered and yet there was always something missing. What was lacking was obvious: a guide to decorating with carpets as demonstrated by the most beautiful rooms done by the very best designers and decorators with whom Stark has worked.

For seventy-five years Stark has celebrated design. We haven't just made carpets. We have worked closely with the most notable designers and decorators to realize their visions, resulting in furnishings for the floor that rival art on the walls. From Stéphane Boudin, whom Jacqueline Kennedy recruited to work on the White House, to Billy Baldwin and Sister Parish, to the hundred designers whose work is featured on the pages of this book, we have collaborated with generations of the most talented creators of magnificent interiors.

Who better, then, to demonstrate the power of a beautiful carpet? By their example in these pages, carpets shine in the quality and chic they lend to a room, in the value, both actual and visual, that they add to any decorating scheme. Room by room, this book takes into consideration exactly what a decorator reviews when evaluating carpets for a space: a room's character and conditions, a rug's relation to other furnishings, color and light, and pragmatic concerns like wear and budget.

From the finest oriental rugs to practical indoor/outdoor carpeting, from the most traditional settings to completely contemporary interiors, there is inspiration and sound decorating advice on every page of this book. It has expanded our own vision of how much a carpet can influence the look and feel of a space. It has also made us appreciate anew the role Stark has played in the decorating world.

Inspired by a Dior scarf, Nadia Stark applied her milliner's eye to carpet and produced a mash-up, Leopard Rose, as stunning today as in the mid-1970s, when it was introduced.

ABOVE In a living room by Steven Gambrel a custom carpet from the Very Antique Collection brings rhythm to the floor like the painting does to the wall, if in a different syncopation (for another view of this room, see pages 50–51).

The final chapter in this book lays out the founding of Stark by our grandfather Arthur and its history over the past seventy-five years. We are proud of his many innovations, of our grandmother Nadia's brilliant idea to combine flowers and exotic animal motifs in the iconic Leopard Rose pattern, and of the enormous contributions our fathers, John and Steven, have made to carrying on the tradition of innovation and artistry for which Stark is known. As the newest generation to be involved with Stark, we are dedicated to continuing that tradition. As we embrace the twenty-first century and implement changes of our own, we will never lose sight of the company's most valuable contribution to decorating, displayed brilliantly in these pages: simply beautiful carpets.

RIGHT A custom hand-knotted area rug is one of the key luxurious elements that designers James Aman and John Meeks used to both complement and offset the traditional Park Avenue architecture of Ashley Stark Kenner's living room (for another view of this room, see pages 88–89).

FOYERS
HALLWAYS
STAIRS

IRST IMPRESSIONS ARE EVERYTHING, GIVING
foyers and their furnishings major influence in the decorative scheme of things, relative to
their size in the house. No matter whether it is grand or modest, a foyer sets the tone for the
rest of the interior. It is where the foot and eye first land before they travel down hallways
and up stairs, along carpets whose job is to welcome and connect.

A foyer carpet is literally a decorative expression of putting one's best foot forward.

Nothing says welcome with more substance and distinction than a one-of-a-kind carpet
such as an antique oriental. For designer Suzanne Kasler, who usually orders custom-
colored new carpets for the rooms she decorates, the foyer is the exception. "It's the one
room where the carpet's role is not so much to coordinate as to stand alone. I actually pre-
fer that the carpet in the front hall not match anything, so I always bring in a found piece."

Oriental rugs, especially those saturated with color like the Persian and Turkish types on
pages 26–29, are transporting. Their richness of hue and pattern alludes to another place and
time, simultaneously grounding and elevating the arrival experience. Carpets in deeper tones
are, moreover, practical; they catch outside dirt before it travels deeper into the house. For all
their finery, oriental carpets are durable if well cared for. After all, they've typically weathered
worse conditions in their lifetime than climate-controlled houses with efficient vacuums.

Quiet orientals like Oushak carpets can lend gravitas to a foyer while imparting a light
touch visually. Even the most magnificent Oushak can feel contemporary, thanks to its subtle
patterning and pale, warm colors. In a foyer with light walls and dark floors such as that on
pages 22–23, the soft palette of an Oushak lends the space a discreetly opulent buoyancy.

Oriental carpets work well in tandem with plain stair runners as on page 31. In this case
the runner is palm grass, a natural fiber similar to sisal—a material as timeless and popular
in classical decorating as oriental rugs. Banding the palm grass gives it the polish it needs to
relate to an antique rug, with the colors of the banding not so much derived from the rug
as inspired by it.

Runners suit handsome entry staircases with fine wood treads.
(On narrower secondary stairs, carpet often extends the full width
of the tread.) They define where feet should fall and cushion the
blow. Banding the runner, like piping a cushion, gives it a degree

Designer Steven Gambrel offsets the curves of
an elliptical stairway with carpet in the Logo
pattern, the squares and palette of which carry the
checkerboard entry floor all the way to the top
of the house.

ABOVE A custom hand-tufted silk carpet provides steady ground for a foyer ringed in fanciful branches by Iain Halliday.

OPPOSITE A zebra hide and a Somali Panther cut-pile runner take the black and white accents in Peter Rogers's apple green entry hall, designed by Rogers and Carl Palasota, in an exotic direction.

of finish and creates an opportunity for color and contrast. On piano keyboard–like stairs, where white risers alternate with dark treads, the banding establishes sharp lines "colored in" by the carpet.

When stairs have both dark treads and risers, the contrast of a stair runner is already built in, so any carpet, with or without a border, lays down a route to follow.

Still, a border can provide further clarification. For a narrow stair in a lodge in Montana (page 30), banding in a cheery red that contrasts with the chocolate brown of the runner and the stairs acts like lights highlighting an airplane aisle, defining the edges of the path.

Nothing enlivens a monochromatic stair hall like a geometric stair runner. Whether the hall itself is classical (page 17 and right) or contemporary, the walls unadorned or not, bold carpeting on the stairs brings modernity and energy to a space that is already about movement. Depending on the design, the pattern can oppose or extend the geometry established by handrail and spindles, dialing the energy up to frisson or down to harmony.

Animal prints are geometry passed through nature's filter. When they appear in stair runners, they have much the same effect on the stair hall as geometric patterns, if a bit softer. For her own house in Massachusetts (pages 42, 43), Liz Caan chose an antelope motif for both a stair runner and an area rug in the hall at the top of the stairs. The muted hues relate to the wall and floor colors, but the unconventional pattern propels the traditional architecture and woodwork of the stair hall into the twenty-first century, providing a context for other contemporary furnishings like a colorful painting and a vivid Lucite console.

Decorators have always had a soft spot for animal prints. The best of them know when to use them sparingly and when to go all in. For the show-stopping apple green entry hall of his New Orleans house (page 19), Peter Rogers embraced two versions of the animal kingdom, a real zebra skin for an area rug and a stair runner in a leopard print, both in black and white to play off the checkerboard floor. If a hall can hold it, drama begets drama.

RIGHT The chain-link pattern of the custom hand-tufted runner in a stair hall by Suzanne Kasler is a riff on the gridded mullions of the windows, softened by curves and an offset figuration.

OVERLEAF The grandeur of a classical double-height entry hall decorated by Marjorie Shushan is reinforced by an antique Oushak carpet. Its pale palette keeps daylight on the move from window to floor to wall to ceiling.

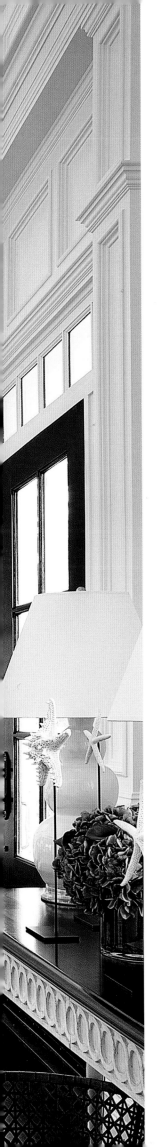

LEFT The grid of a custom flatweave rug in a spacious entry hall decorated by Alexa Hampton echoes the pattern of the wall paneling.

ABOVE In an entry hall of buffed and polished surfaces that reflect light, Noel Jeffrey selected a custom Tibetan carpet that offers a place for the eye to rest.

ABOVE A Persian carpet in bold reds, yellows, and blues balances the strong yellow of papered walls in an entry hall by Amy Thebault.

OPPOSITE In a pale entry hall by Solis Betancourt & Sherrill, the border of a creamy stair runner picks up the blue ground of an antique Tabriz rug whose warm medallions connect to the oak flooring.

OVERLEAF An antique northwest Persian carpet in a hallway by Timothy Corrigan is a visual and practical bridge to a red brick terrace furnished with seating upholstered in blue.

ABOVE In the back stairway of a mountain lodge decorated by Amy Thebault, the red leather binding on the custom Wilton carpet perks up the brown-on-brown layering of a runner on the stairs.

OPPOSITE Palm grass is at home in even the grandest spaces, especially when finished with a leather border and paired with oriental rugs, as it is here in a traditional stair hall that Timothy Corrigan hung with portraits.

OPPOSITE The white leather border and subtle weave of this stair runner in the Joshua pattern, held in place by brass rods, are an elegant foil to the drama of yellow walls as deep as egg yolk in this stair hall by Lee Bierly and Christopher Drake.

ABOVE In this all-white entry hall by Calder Design Group, a red carpet lives up to its traditional role, unfurling majestically up the stairs.

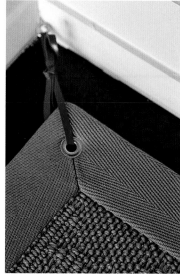

LEFT AND ABOVE Leather laces threaded through eyelets in the border of a sisal rug, Indochine from the Charlotte Moss Collection, keep it in place in this rustic yet elegant hall of a country house she decorated.

OPPOSITE Suzanne Kasler selected a subtle tone-on-tone Cleon Stria in truffle from the Thomas Jayne Collection, to pick up where the variegated stone pavers leave off, in a soft version for the stairs.

LEFT John Anderson chose a custom overdyed carpet to brighten a wood-paneled entry hall in a house in San Francisco, its silvery hue a reminder of the iconic local fog.

ABOVE The subtle gray stripe of carpet in the Les Millerais pattern unites with stair risers and stringers in the same tone to create a quiet path winding through a wildly wallpapered entry hall by Lindsey Coral Harper.

IKAT

In the late 1960s and early '70s geometric carpets set floors ablaze. They were bold, they were colorful, they expressed energy and optimism. Ikat carpets are this century's version— also bright and bold but featuring patterns that are at once more natural and more exotic.

On the heels of the first moon landing, science ruled, making geometrics in tune with their time. Ikats and similar patterns rooted in ancient cultures tap the diversity of our age, the interconnectedness of our world, and our need for softer edges in an era dominated by technology.

Though the name may be derived from an Indonesian word, ikat patterns turn up in textiles from China, Japan, Africa, Central Asia, and Southeast Asian locales like Malaysia and Bali. On a trip to Istanbul, designer Charlotte Moss was captivated by vintage ikat silks, seeing in their strong patterns and saturated colors the potential for wonderfully rich carpets. Thus her Passport Collection for Stark was born.

In a traditional interior, hand-knotted wool ikat carpets deliver gravitas with a big dose of *joie*. In a modern interior, ikat carpets temper the man-made with warmth and texture, their colors often a broader and deeper expression of a strict palette.

LEFT The rich colors and blurred-edge patterns that characterize ikat carpets make them a favorite for modernizing traditional interiors and spicing up contemporary spaces. These four examples only touch on the infinite range of colors and patterns that Stark offers.

RIGHT Geometrics were to the 1960s and '70s what ikat patterns are to our time: bold, colorful, and expressive.

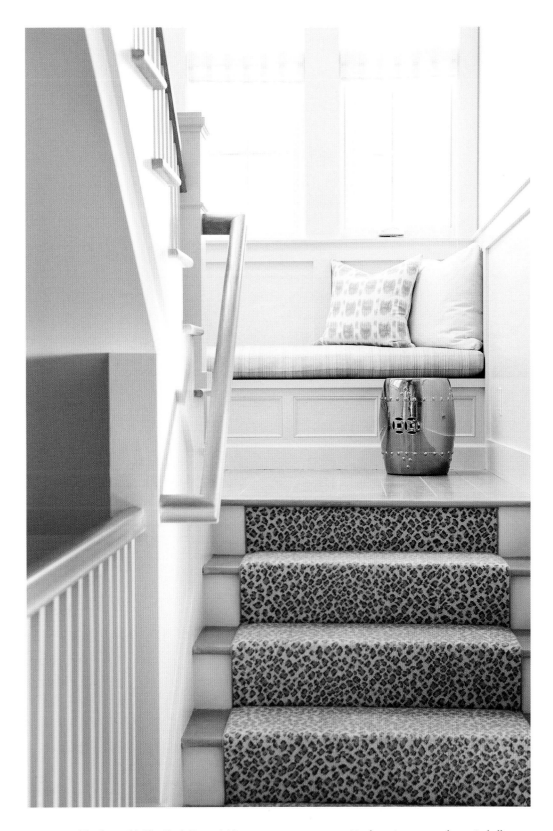

OPPOSITE The foyer of Ashley Stark Kenner's New York apartment, designed by James Aman and John Meeks, is a study in gold and silver, with an ikat rug from the Noor Collection providing the cooler tone and predominant pattern.

ABOVE The tight pattern of a runner in the Lynx pattern suits the intimate scale of a stair hall in a house decorated by Lucas Studio.

OVERLEAF For the stair runner and upstairs hall rug of a house with traditional detailing in Massachusetts, designer Liz Caan chose a wild card of a hard-wearing carpet, Antilocarpa in silver.

LIVING ROOMS

For all the laments in the twenty-first century about the decline of manners and restraint, there has been an upside at home: the living room is less about a stiff viewing and more about contented living. In only the most reserved houses is this space designated for guests and occasions. Still, no matter the tone, regardless of style, living rooms share one thing in common. They remain, in most houses, both the largest room and the place where decorating takes the highest road. When it comes to carpet, that translates into a challenge.

Determining carpets for the living room involves an equation—space + budget + approach—but no set formula. The most common course is to have the rug take the lead in the decorating scheme. The bigger the room and the better the quality of carpet, the more likely that the rug will set the mood and dictate the palette.

Designer Bunny Williams turns to antique carpets for palette inspiration because of the unusual color combinations she finds in them. Custom carpets are designer Suzanne Kasler's go-to. "Once the floor plan is set, we start talking about concepts and looking at rugs. There are so many great options today because anything can be created. A client being inspired by a pattern or a color gives us a design direction." The carpet is the anchor and the starting point of all of Kasler's projects.

Designer Jeffrey Bilhuber is also a fan of custom carpets—"They're more flexible, meaning more fun"—but for his projects, the carpet is the magic force that arrives at the end, with the power and the responsibility to unite and clarify. "We ask the carpet to connect all the dots and to illuminate the furniture plan."

If the definition of a modern living room is a space that is warm, hospitable, and inviting, then it must have intimate groupings. Carpets, working in tandem with furniture arrangements, achieve that. Area rugs, new and antique, factor heavily in Bilhuber-decorated living rooms. Much as he likes the carpet to ground a room, he never wants it to obscure the quality of what lies beneath. When a room has beautiful floors, he uses separate rugs as islands in a sea, to establish a series of conversational pools.

To visually link his rug islands, Bilhuber often literally cuts them from the same cloth. He'll search out an antique carpet larger than the room itself and then consciously cut it down. What might

In a living room with walls paneled in a cool mint green, Thomas Jayne used an antique rug in beautiful shades of pink and plum to bring out the warm tones in the traditional furnishings.

seem radical is actually a time-honored tradition of repurposing. "My client Peter Jennings taught me that there is a long history of carpets being recut and resized over time. Mending and repairing is not off-putting, it's part of the allure."

Of course, not everyone can start with a palatial antique carpet. Layering fine area rugs atop an expanse of carpet such as sisal is a well-established technique for addressing a large living room affordably. "A sisal carpet provides a neutral ground that pulls a big room together," says designer Charlotte Moss. "The risk is that it can look a little bland. By dropping a rug on top, you have a chance to make the color palette of the room cohesive"—or easily shift the color scheme and atmosphere. In summer Moss like to swap out an oriental area rug in her own living room for a cotton dhurrie. Instantly, the room downshifts to a more relaxed disposition.

Moss uses a living room rug as a tool. If the upholstery fabric is dynamic, she uses the carpet to calm things down. If a room leans monochromatic, then the rug becomes tonal. If a room needs an injection of energy, a carpet can provide it. If a room is filled with important pieces of furniture and art, a rug can dress it down. "Every element in a room cannot be formal," says Moss. "A sisal rug allows everyone to drop their shoulders."

Rugs are not necessarily the first things that she puts before a client but they are never the last. Budget walks hand in hand with design development. "Sometimes, when people are in love with furniture or art, they neglect the rug and run out of money for the floor," she says. "I will never let that happen because a rug can truly make or break a room. The greatest furniture is cheapened by a bad rug."

Conversely, a splendid rug can sustain a living room while furnishings join it as the budget allows. It provides a place to lounge and lends, in a single surface, great dimension to decorating. It puts something of lasting value in a room. Best of all, a fine carpet is the most portable treasure. You can feel secure in investing in one because you can take it with you.

PRECEDING PAGES The overscaled yet fanciful pattern of an Aubusson rug suits the grand proportions and elegant furnishings in a living room by Suzanne Rheinstein.

LEFT An antique Sarouk rug atop cobalt blue wall-to-wall carpeting knits together the blues and reds in a living room by McGeehan Design.

OVERLEAF Steven Gambrel plays off a fireplace surround's variegated marble with a custom carpet from the Very Antique Collection.

LEFT A trellis of ribbons and roses woven into a pale pink custom Savonnerie rug sets the tone for other pastel furnishings in a living room by Michael Simon.

ABOVE The tendrils and blossoms of a custom Aubusson rug from the Veronica Collection reinforce the fresh spring feel of a living room by Linda Ruderman.

In a living room by Markham Roberts the black Flower Sepia carpet reads as modern chic while its floral bouquets link it, like the fringed sofa, to a Victorian time.

OPPOSITE In a richly decorated living room by Michael Smith, a custom Alpuhara rug adds yet another pattern while its palette of ivory and blues counters darker tones.

ABOVE In Woody Allen's living room, decorated by Steven Shadley, an antique Aubusson carpet partners with walls in similar warm tones to offset the deeper shades of velvet chairs and walnut bookcases.

Alexa Hampton used a custom hand-knotted
carpet of soft blue and warm brown to tie together
the wall and sofa colors and to introduce pattern
to balance the solids.

OPPOSITE In a living room by Trisha Reger the tracery in a custom handmade rug complements the delicate form of the coffee table and the fine details in the chair upholstery fabric.

ABOVE Witmer Design used a pale custom handmade rug to establish a more intimate seating area within a lofty living room with dark walls and floor.

ORIENTAL

An oriental rug has always been a statement—of quality, of luxury, of cosmopolitan taste and timelessness. The barest of rooms can look dressed to the nines so long as it features a glorious oriental rug.

Oriental is an all-encompassing term covering all of Asia, from Turkey to China, enveloping Iran, Central Asia, Pakistan, India, Nepal, and Tibet en route. The diversity of patterns in oriental rugs, from floral to geometric to single-direction prayer rugs, is a direct reflection of the multiplicity of sources from which they come. Patterns are indigenous not just to countries but also to particular regions and tribes.

For some people, only an antique will do. To embrace that audience, Stark brought the Darius Collection of antique rugs, assembled over the course of four generations, under its wing. But even the most generous budget cannot always accommodate an antique, especially when the size is large. For that, there are reproduction orientals that capture all the subtlety and finesse of antique rugs.

When the advances of new mills meet the talents of traditional weavers, together they can produce carpets with a high/low weave that imparts a sense of wear along with a subtle palette that mimics the fading that comes with age. Never have new rugs been so expert at masquerading as old, yet their fresh fibers will wear well for years. Thus a treasure for future generations is born.

LEFT Inspired by museum documents as well as actual antique rugs, reproduction carpets know no limits. Among them, clockwise from left, are an oriental in soft green, a Kelim in traditional reds and blues, a Persian with stylized flowers and vines, and a Savonnerie in a classic pastel palette.

RIGHT An ad from the 1960s references Stark's long tradition of roaming the world in search of the finest carpets.

PRECEDING PAGES The custom French linen ivory carpet in a living room by Nancy Braithwaite lends a traditionally furnished room a thoroughly modern air.

ABOVE The sisal carpet in Bruce Shostak's living room is a reminder that, in spite of the presence of fine antiques, this is a country house.

OPPOSITE For his own living room, Darryl Carter used a Saranac carpet in butte tan and white upholstery fabric to keep the focus on furniture form.

In a living room by Avondale Design where
a grand piano only adds to the weightiness of
the wood bookcases and beamed ceiling, the
light tone-on-tone Parkshim carpet provides
a welcome counterbalance.

OPPOSITE In a living room by Eberlein Design, an Everest area rug with a coordinating border behaves like the wallpaper, providing overall pattern while letting natural wood shine.

ABOVE To calm a living room as richly decorated as a Victorian parlor, the Jeffrey Design Group turned to a custom Wilton carpet.

OVERLEAF LEFT The arcs carved into a custom hand-tufted carpet subtly complement the Art Deco spirit that Susan Winton-Feinberg of Walter Herz Interiors brings to a glamorous living room.

OVERLEAF RIGHT The swirls in a custom Tibetan carpet pick up the accents of gold that enliven a rich red living room by Bebe Winkler.

PRECEDING PAGES For a family-friendly living area in Elton John's house, designed by Martyn Lawrence Bullard, a patchwork cowhide rug is as rough and tumble, and indestructible, as a leather sectional.

ABOVE Tony Ingrao and Randy Kemper established distinct seating areas in Donny Deutsch's living room with the help of twin custom cowhide carpets in a brick patchwork.

OPPOSITE A custom mohair rug adds another layer of softness to the leather, fur, and linen in a living room by Ann Holden.

ABOVE AND OPPOSITE Planes of solid color and material, including a
custom hand-tufted area rug that warms a stone floor, are the decorative elements
in the open-plan living area of a modern house by architects Todd Williams
and Billie Tsien.

A Tibetan rug from the Thomas Jayne Collection
maintains the symmetry of a room by the designer
while its starbursts bring levity to the formal
arrangement.

OPPOSITE Sherrill Canet designed a jazzy rug—the Bargello pattern in silver—to augment the syncopation of brass accents in a living room with deep blue walls.

ABOVE The bold pattern and coloration of a handmade ikat rug lends spice to a living room by Judy King that is dominated by quieter natural materials.

OVERLEAF Barry Goralnick designed the Wavy Gravy hand-tufted Tibetan carpet specifically to complement mid-century modern furnishings like those in this living room.

ABOVE The brisk pattern and muted colors (undyed sheep wool) of a kilim rug from the Giza Collection suit a living room by Kelter Schwartz that is dominated by natural woods.

OPPOSITE The rigorously consistent solids and voids of a sculpted carpet from the Dorjee Collection offset the irregular pockets of a weighty coffee table of burled wood in a living room by Marie Flanigan.

OVERLEAF The plushness of a custom hand-knotted area rug in Ashley Stark Kenner's living room, designed by James Aman and John Meeks, extends the sense of luxury established by antique fauteuils and silk tiger-patterned upholstery.

ABOVE AND OPPOSITE The ribs of a Zavala sisal carpet extend the fringe of
an upholstered bench and bring welcome texture to a living room with smooth
white walls by Carrier and Company.

Jeffrey Bilhuber used rugs in the Sorrento pattern bound with leather laces to create conversational islands within the vast living room of John and Andrea Stark's penthouse apartment.

ABOVE Wall-to-wall sisal, like the gray-stained wood wall planking and white canvas slipcovers, suits the casual living room Bruce Bierman designed for a house on Fire Island.

OPPOSITE A zebra hide outlined in black and laid atop a Natura sisal carpet in silver delivers an extra visual treat at the base of glass coffee tables in a living room by Triangle Interiors.

OPPOSITE Except for the wall surfaces, pattern is everywhere in this interior by Mark Hampton, including the textured Clay Stria sisal carpet in almond from the Alexa Hampton Collection.

ABOVE Like the bobbin chairs in a driftwood finish, Charlotte Moss's Shangri La woven sisal carpet softens the straight lines of a living room by Munger Interiors.

PRECEDING PAGES Wild things are overhead (an antler chandelier) and underfoot (Antelope Ax carpet in chocolate) in an otherwise traditionally furnished great room by Amy Thebault.

ABOVE The subtle stripe in the Antelope Ax pattern comes across as a plush and exotic version of wide-plank flooring in a blue living room by M Interiors.

OPPOSITE The abstracted leopard pattern of Namir carpeting, along with a fur throw and textiles in lively motifs, temper the formality of a traditionally paneled living room decorated by Markham Roberts.

OVERLEAF In a space as colorful and eclectic as this living room by Thomas Britt, the floor would be lost without a coat—like the Linen Panther carpet—that measures up.

ABOVE Like the bread of a sandwich with spicy fillings, the Arabesque carpet in Ashley Stark Kenner's den is a twin of the wood ceiling inset in color, texture, and size.

OPPOSITE In a living room by Martyn Lawrence Bullard that is a free-wheeling mélange of form and pattern, a rug pieced together from zebra hides seems tame.

ABOVE The small-scale white-and-brown grid of a Les Damiers carpet knits together dark wood walls and a white marble fireplace in a living room by Jan Showers.

OPPOSITE The tight, labyrinthine squares of a wool bouclé Park Square carpet in white and gray provide a consistent geometric foundation for the many and varied furnishings in this living room.

OPPOSITE Jan Showers chose the Ellipse carpet from the Sherrill Canet Collection to give a calm living room a dose of snappy attitude.

ABOVE The interlocking Ys of the Yogi pattern from the David Hicks Collection lend extra dynamism to an already mod living room by Kapito Muller.

OVERLEAF Howard Slatkin's design for his hand-tufted Liliane carpet captures the same lighthearted yet luxurious esprit as that of the eighteenth-century Venetian mirror he hung above the fireplace in a New York apartment.

STUDIES
LIBRARIES

After the kitchen, studies and librar-
ies are often the most favored place in the house. More intimate than the living room, more
communal than a bedroom, more comfortable than the kitchen, they are where occupants
choose to tuck in to read, watch TV, surf the Internet, have a nightcap, and if they're lucky,
curl up by the fire.

Cozy by nature, these spaces take on a hospitable style that carpets are essential in
supporting.

Wood-paneled walls are the standard bearers of the traditional study. In rooms with
honey-colored wood like chestnut, a carpet in the same tone, like that on pages 118–19,
completes the sense of being enveloped by warmth. Even the pattern of the carpet and the
subtle variation in color suggest the grain found in the wood. In other rooms with paneling
of similar hue, a paler carpet lifts the atmosphere while still providing a cocooning effect.

Studies and libraries lined with darker shelving call for different treatment. Designer
Timothy Corrigan opted for a carpet in the Blakeville pattern in cream and light blue to temper the sobriety of wood shelving stained a deep walnut (pages 114–15). Together with a white
ceiling, the pale carpet also balances the abundant sunlight that is a constant for this room in
Los Angeles. In another link to nature, the carpet's hues place a cloud-studded sky underfoot.

As bridges between the public and private areas of a house, studies are often the truest
expression of individual style. Charlotte Moss's sitting room, seen opposite, could not be
more personal. It is filled with photographs and drawings, books and *objets*, antique furniture and favorite mementos. Pulling it all together is a palette of white and duck-egg blue
that shifts in value as it moves from hand-stenciled walls to curtains to carpet. The floor
covering here is a custom-colored wall-to-wall variation on a floral theme that contributes
to the feel of a totally feminine, pulled-together room.

A study by Scot Meacham Wood (page 126) could not be more masculine, though via
an unconventional design vocabulary. A glass desk fairly disappears amid the dark folds
of a Coromandel screen and under the weight of paintings and
books. Pulling it all together is a hand-knotted ikat carpet in rich
yet varied hues—deep gray to pale blue—that bridge the gap
between black lacquer and bright brass and perfectly offset a

The custom Wilton carpet in decorator Charlotte
Moss's study is a densely patterned variation on a
theme: floral motifs in blue and white.

chair lacquered red. The carpet's pattern is as unexpected and inspiring as a plaid seat on a Chippendale chair.

A study can swing decoratively from maximal to minimal but libraries are, in the visual sense, consistently busy spaces. The dense patterning of book-lined rooms presents a particular decorating condition. One can either go all in and increase the density or step back to counterbalance it. A carpet is one of the easiest ways to tip the scale in either direction.

The libraries on pages 116–17 are perfect examples of more is more. The classical motifs of the carpet that lines a room by Charlotte Moss sit well with the traditional moldings, window treatments, and furnishings while the bolder scale of its pattern casts the room in a more contemporary light. In Mario Buatta's deep rose library, carpet in an overall ocelot pattern grounds a room flying high on chinoiserie and tiger stripes. A needlepoint rug laid atop the wall-to-wall in front of the hearth both protects the carpet and pulls in the colors of the walls and fireplace surround.

Patterned carpets are great counterweights to solid elements of a room. Garrow Kedigian and Vicente Wolf both elected to dip libraries they were designing in delicious shades of blue and both turned to geometric patterns for the carpet. In Kedigian's room (page 120), the overscaled Greek key on a ground of ivory lends a traditionally furnished space an elegant modernity. The tighter geometric pattern in Wolf's library (page 131) is a nod to the maze of knowledge available in books so tightly packed into shelves that they form their own decorative motif.

Patterned carpets also supply the perfect foundation for studies that double as family rooms. Given the different ages and activities the room hosts, from homework and office work to game and snack times, a carpet with an overall dense pattern is not only the most forgiving, in terms of wear and spills, but also the most flexible. With the carpet run wall to wall, as in the den by Victoria Hagan on page 133, it's easy to rearrange the furniture to accommodate any form of work or play without disrupting the room's overall decoration.

A pale blue-and-white area rug in the Blakeville pattern works with a white ceiling to balance walls lined with dark wood shelving in a library by Timothy Corrigan.

ABOVE The palette of a custom Wilton tile-patterned carpet pulls together camel-colored walls, creamy woodwork, and darker furnishings in a library by Charlotte Moss.

OPPOSITE An even-tempered carpet in the Ocelot pattern is the perfect support for exuberant and exotic furnishings in a rose-colored library by Mario Buatta.

OVERLEAF In a study by Bunny Williams, the warm tones of a custom rug extend the honey-colored paneling while the russet stripe threads together the many red accents in the room.

ABOVE The Greek key pattern of the Tibetan rug in Garrow Kedigian's library is as striking as the high-gloss blue walls, yet its pale ground adds welcome softness.

OPPOSITE A Tibetan carpet in Steven and Candice Stark's study, designed by Trisha Reger, sets the tone for other furnishings in cream, beige, and camel.

RIGHT The strié of a Tillbury carpet chosen by Jesse Carrier and Mara Miller for this study adds texture without competing with the bolder textiles of curtains and upholstery.

OVERLEAF LEFT In a traditional library by Cullman & Kravis, the Box Velour tattersall carpet is an unexpected yet well-suited classic.

OVERLEAF RIGHT The sprays of dots in the Antelope Ax carpet are perfect complements to the graceful X-braces of a desk in a study by Jan Showers.

OPPOSITE A custom hand-knotted ikat rug with unusual hues and patterning lays the groundwork for an eclectically furnished study by Scot Meacham Wood.

ABOVE A round Sloan carpet with leather binding sets the furniture free from conventional arrangement in a study by Jamie Drake.

GEOMETRIC

Geometric carpet patterns seem utterly contemporary, at the very least twentieth century. During the late 1960s and early '70s they blanketed interiors, especially those done by the man most associated with them, British decorator David Hicks. But many of the patterns are thousands of years old, even those known as iconic "Hicks" motifs.

It turns out that Stark Carpet and Hicks were rooting through the same source at the same time and pulling from it the same patterns. A hundred years after its publication in 1856, Owen Jones's authoritative tome, *The Grammar of Ornament*, was a gold mine yielding patterns that set the decorating world on fire. Classic Hicks designs like Wye, Cairo, and Hexagon, and classic Stark patterns like Key Stria, Harvey, Hadera, and Egyptian Lattice, were all born of the same page, Plate LIX, in the section of Jones's book on Chinese ornament.

What both Hicks and Stark tapped into was the winning attributes of geometrics: exuberance combined with uniformity. Like classic tile patterns, geometric carpets can bring to a floor a layer of interest that is engaging without being distracting. Cut-pile and bouclé geometric carpets are practical and flexible and endlessly varied, but most of all they're fun.

LEFT Contemporary colors may be tamer than when these carpets were first introduced, but the patterns are now classics. Clockwise from top left: Large Hexagon in Desert Night, Beatrice Blue, Balara Surf, Parkshim Golden, Bray in Surf, Jeter in Quartz, a hand-tufted interlocking-diamond pattern from the David Hicks Collection, Blackburn Riverbank, Octagon.

RIGHT The bold patterns and bright colors of geometric carpets were a major factor in propelling chic interiors in a whole new direction in the 1970s.

ABOVE A geometric carpet in the Logo pattern provides the perfect balance for the dense patterning of shelves filled with books in a library by Austin Harrelson.

OPPOSITE In an otherwise all-blue library by Vicente Wolf, a carpet in the Carabello pattern creates an intriguing mazelike effect underfoot.

OPPOSITE A custom Wilton carpet strikes just the right balance between pattern and solid, rustic and refined, in a Montana den decorated by Markham Roberts.

ABOVE A Wilton carpet in Wye, a pattern of interlocking Ys, provides a forgiving, family-friendly base in a den by Victoria Hagan.

OVERLEAF LEFT Like a field of silver filings, the carpet in a study by Avondale Design Studio pulls together multiple accents in chrome and stainless steel.

OVEREAF RIGHT Mojo Stumer Associates used a custom Tibetan carpet with a linocutlike pattern of wavy lines to relieve the solid blocks of white brick, wood panels, and gray upholstery in this study.

PAGES 136–37 A carpet in the Braddock pattern references the grid of streets that a study by Mark Hampton overlooks.

DINING ROOMS

IF THERE IS ONE IMMUTABLE THING ABOUT a dining room, it is the presence of a table. Rare is the arrangement that departs from a central table surrounded by chairs. And though some tables don occasional accessories and all certainly get dressed for dinner, most spend the better part of their lives as plain expanses that dominate the room.

All the more reason, then, to introduce variety and texture, and quiet, via the carpet.

"Dining rooms typically have so many hard surfaces," says designer Katie Ridder, "yet they are the one place in the house where upwards of eight people may be trying to have conversations simultaneously. That makes the acoustical benefits of a carpet essential." For that reason alone the carpet should be of a generous size, large enough to comfortably "float" the dining table (or tables) and chairs on an island that covers most of the hard flooring.

Dining room carpets dampen sound not only by muffling conversation but also by cushioning the furniture. A high-quality carpet, new or old, can tolerate guests pushing chairs back from the table as well as spills, which are always a concern in eating areas. Adds Ridder, "The common worry is that any carpet under a dining room table will be ruined. In fact, a sturdy antique carpet in good condition holds up well. And stains, which can appear in any room, can be cleaned and are less noticeable in a patterned carpet such as an oriental."

Patterns of all kinds, whether in the texture of the weave or in coloration and design, are a good choice for dining rooms and not just because they better disguise a drop of wine or a sprinkling of crumbs. A patterned carpet introduces a welcome divergence from the second-largest horizontal plane in the room: the smooth top of the dining table. As with a wild meadow bordering a glassy pond, the visual interest is in the contrast.

No matter how varied the pattern, carpets in today's dining rooms are veering in a lighter direction than ever before. Dining rooms with oriental carpets in deep jewel tones establish a certain decorum, sobriety even, that rooms with paler carpets seem to lift. Lighter carpets simply project a more lighthearted attitude. Moreover, they brighten a room that is most often used after dark. When chandeliers and sconces dimmed to match candlelight are the only lighting, it's easier for guest and server alike to find their way on a field that reflects more light than it absorbs.

In a dining room by Alex Papachristidis, a handmade reproduction of an antique Samarkand carpet brightens the wood grain–papered walls and cues the appliqués on the chair seats and backs.

Ashley Stark Kenner's Manhattan dining room (page 163), decorated by James Aman and John Meeks, is a perfect example of the new light and modern paradigm. Underneath the whitewashed tree-trunk pedestals of the table is a patchwork carpet of cowhide. The grid of the seams offsets the irregular form of the table base, and its skin is a rough counterpoint to the delicate hand-painted wallpaper. Not only is the custom cowhide carpet unexpected and oddly luxurious, but it's also durable and low-maintenance.

When it comes to selecting carpets for heavily used, family-friendly dining areas like breakfast rooms and kitchen nooks, Katie Ridder turns to a type of carpeting that has vastly improved in quality and variety in recent times: indoor/outdoor sisal. "It's indestructible and easy to dress up by binding the edges in wide cotton tape that refers to the decorating scheme of the room," she says. Gone are the days when indoor/outdoor carpeting evoked cheap patio coverings.

Dressing a quite formal dining room in the least precious carpet might seem unorthodox, but it is a tradition of great English country houses that designer Jeffrey Bilhuber, for one, applauds. Furnishing a stately dining room with a humble natural fiber carpet "is a way to keep the eye above the horizon of the tabletop, where all the splendor is," he says. Rush, hemp, and sisal are the durable antithesis of fragile materials like porcelain and glass, their textures dull and rough against the luster of silver and the sparkle of crystal.

The contrast is precisely the point. Says Bilhuber, "No matter how exquisitely the dining room may be appointed, it should feel warm and welcoming. A natural fiber carpet, by tempering the formality, puts people at ease." It's exactly the approach he took to decorate the dining room in Andrea and John Stark's penthouse apartment (page 161). The light fixture comprises dazzling branches of crystals, the curtains are embellished with discs of abalone and mother-of-pearl, the walls are covered in a silk-and-wool damask, and the table is a Louis XVI antique. But underneath it all is a carpet woven of rush, providing a platform—noble in tradition yet humble in material—for all the finery.

PRECEDING PAGES Margaret Kirkland chose a Sultanabad rug in light hues to support the relaxed tone set by a painted dining table, oak chairs, and an iron pendant fixture.

RIGHT A custom hand-tufted Octagon carpet from the David Hicks Collection quietly adds further texture to a dining area by Katie Ridder, where pattern, color, and form are exuberantly expressed.

ABOVE A sisal carpet woven in the Natura diamond pattern partners well with cream and celadon wallpaper and other light furnishings to make the dark mahogany pedestal table the star in a dining room by Ashley Whittaker.

OPPOSITE Carpet in the vine-strewn Villandry pattern extends the floral fantasy of a dining room by Mario Buatta done up in macaron pastels.

ANIMAL

Stark introduced four animal patterns—Design Zebra, Ocelot, Somali Panther, and Leopard—during the same period that geometric patterns debuted, the late 1960s. After the drab postwar '50s, it was time to go wild.

Interiors flaunting exotic animals had once been the province of big-game hunters who prized animal skins more as trophies than floor coverings. Animal-patterned velvet pile carpets allowed decorators to take interiors on a different kind of safari. Leopard in particular threw down a new gauntlet. Socialite C. Z. Guest used it in the hall of Templeton, her Long Island mansion, to chicly camouflage muddy paw prints. Jenna Lyons, creative director at J. Crew, goes one step further in asserting its practicality. "As far as I'm concerned, leopard is a neutral."

Antelope, a pattern launched in the 1970s and exclusive to Stark, has become the star neutral of our time. The warmth of its palette and the allure of its pattern, at once rhythmic and untamed, make for a winning carpet. It turns up in kids' rooms as an adventurous co-conspirator, in game rooms as a promoter of cutting loose, in studies as a flight of fancy, even in dining rooms as the perfect disguiser of spills and as a magic vehicle for unleashing great dinner parties.

LEFT No other carpet company is so associated with animal patterns as Stark. Clockwise from top left: Zebra Cut Pile in Black/White, Siberian in Gold, Bobcat in Beach, Mini Leopard in Black, Antelope Ax, and Leopard Rose Petite.

RIGHT Stark's animal print carpets were an instant rage when they debuted in 1969 and are still go-to patterns for their graphic dynamism.

OPPOSITE The delicate pattern of a custom Tibetan carpet offsets the baronial furniture in a dining room by Steven Gambrel.

ABOVE The symmetry and formality of a dining room by Robert Brown is leavened by an Antelope Ax carpet.

LEFT The diamond weave of the Natura sisal carpet echoes the pattern of the wood ceiling's fine moldings in a dining room by Cullman & Kravis.

OVERLEAF LEFT A custom Ionia carpet in a dining room by Meadowbank Designs is a simpler variation on a theme established by the chairs' slipcover fabric.

OVERLEAF RIGHT Trisha Reger used a custom flatweave rug to knit together tones of driftwood and blue in a dining room by the shore.

For ease of access and maintenance, Massucco Warner Miller chose to run Pecola sisal right up to the baseboard beneath the window seat of a casual dining area dressed in other natural materials like caning, linen, and wood.

OPPOSITE In the dining area of Steven and Candice Stark's apartment, designed by Trisha Reger, the rich texture of a Mongolian sheepskin rug works double time: to set off the glossy Macassar ebony table and to connect to the ribbed walls of Venetian plaster.

ABOVE With his Dashes rug, designer Barry Goralnick sought to update traditional animal-patterned carpets, employing irregular swatches of lustrous silk fiber to create patches of "hide."

LEFT The subtle weave and sandy tones of a wool Clay Stria carpet from the Alexa Hampton Collection support the beachy scheme of a dining room by Carrier and Company.

OVERLEAF LEFT A custom Wilton carpet run wall to wall takes on the look of a lively mosaic floor, absent the cacophonous hardness, in John and Andrea Stark's breakfast room.

OVERLEAF RIGHT In the dining room Jeffrey Bilhuber decorated for John and Andrea Stark, the lines of a custom carpet woven of rush echo the horizontal stripes in the grouping of paintings by Kenneth Noland.

ABOVE A carpet from the Noor Collection, featuring a blend of wool and silk fibers that reference the irregular slub of the wallcovering, defines the dining area of an interior by Amy Vermillion.

OPPOSITE In Ashley Stark Kenner's dining room, designed by James Aman and John Meeks, cowhide cut into squares and stitched into a large carpet lays the groundwork for furnishings that range from natural to formal.

OVERLEAF A custom hand-tufted carpet in the Athena pattern from the Charles Allen Collection simultaneously accentuates the straight lines of the furnishings and contributes a bold and irregular pattern to the dining area of an apartment by CAD International.

ENTERTAINMENT
SPACES

People may appreciate the most beautiful parts of a house, but they gravitate to the fun parts. Kids cut loose in the playrooms, teens take over the pool houses and billiard rooms, grown-ups savor the sunrooms, the whole family loves dens and screening rooms and yachts. The recreation or relaxation that takes place in these spaces may be the primary draw but without sympathetic decorating to support them, these rooms would suffer the greatest indignity of all: being wasted space.

The carpets in these rooms are as varied as their functions, though the conditions of each type of space have no small influence on the kind of carpet that is suitable. Ringed by windows and infused with light and air, sunrooms call for pale rugs to keep the swirl of freshness in motion. A dark carpet in such a space would feel like the bottom fell out of the room. Likewise a light carpet in a screening room, a space that's meant to be a dark womb, would be a distraction.

With more exposure to the outside than any other interior space, sunrooms present a decorating opportunity to reach out to nature and invite it in. A carpet strewn with flowers or ferns as in the room on pages 172–73, allows the sunroom to become an extension of a garden beyond. A pale blue rug in a game room with a view of the sea (pages 170–71) draws it much closer, allowing its occupants to get a taste of walking on water.

Screening rooms present conditions at the opposite end of the spectrum. They are chic caves where the primary light is meant to come from the screen itself. Specifying deeper hues for the furnishings allows the room to fast-forward into darkness, though when lighting is dimmed, all colors recede into the shadows.

All screening rooms share the need for carpets to be an acoustical aid in dampening noise, making a plush cut the most commonly called for type of carpet. But rooms that are used irregularly and are fully hidden behind a door are perfect places to cut loose stylistically. Given that movies are about fantasy, here is a chance to escape convention and delve into some glamorous or eccentric pattern, as in the room on the top of page 186.

The glory days of movie theaters, when they were treated like opulent palaces, are ripe sources for inspiration. As are favorite places from a memorable trip. The fireplace and gray flannel upholstery in a screening room by Trisha Reger (pages 184–85)

The lively patterning of the custom hand-knotted carpet Margaret Kirkland chose for a playroom provides a fun and practical platform for all kinds of activities.

OPPOSITE AND ABOVE Like sand blown across the floor of a colorful cabana on the beach, Whirl, a wavy seagrass carpet, amplifies the air of fantasy Alessandra Branca created for a tented pool house.

OVERLEAF Ribs and ripples of shades of blue in an Ipswich carpet are a reminder that the living area of a game room decorated by Liz Caan is surrounded by water.

make for incredibly cozy viewing, but it's the tartan carpeting that sends the room into a fling with the Scottish Highlands.

Game and billiard rooms share the entertainment prerogatives of screening rooms except that they are less insular; both natural and artificial light come into play. And instead of all eyes looking up and facing one direction, they are commonly focused on table height. In such conditions, carpeting in bright colors or large-scale patterns could take the eyes off the prize.

Usually it's the pool table itself that cues the carpet. In a Palm Beach billiard room (page 182) that glows with pier mirrors and gilded-bronze sconces, the ornately carved table is set off by a golden carpet that resembles nothing less than watered silk. In a billiard room of equally grand proportions but far less formal attitude (page 181), an antelope print playfully carpets the floor.

If a poolroom is typically an inward-looking space, one most often used in the cooler months, a pool house is quite the opposite. In a room designed for easy transition between indoors and out, the carpet must be prepared both to embrace nature visually and to handle its incursions—of water and sand mostly.

Sisal is the preferred treatment for such conditions. The highest grade of the natural fiber is used for carpets that are strong, durable, and, thanks to its resistance to static electricity, kind to bare feet. Hard-wearing and affordable, sisal comes in weaves and colors that seem to emerge from the natural environment. In a pool house by Alessandra Branca (pages 168–69), the waters appear to have just receded, leaving ripples in the carpet.

Waves are naturally graphic and a perfect motif for yachts, which are either riding them or looking out at them. Given the constant panorama of nature that yachts provide, an abstracted pattern that supports but does not compete with the surroundings, such as overscaled nautical ropes (page 190–91) seems appropriate for the saloon's carpet. Regardless of motif, safety issues dictate that the carpet sit flush with any other floor material. When one's stability may already be rocky, there's no need to provide something extra to trip over. Better a dense, soft surface to buffer any pitching and swaying and to invite the lounging that yachts are so conducive to.

RIGHT In a contemporary take on a traditional conservatory, the needlepoint carpet in a sunroom decorated by Bruce Bierman features sprays of fern fronds.

OVERLEAF A Ravi sisal area rug atop a stone floor lends a breezy indoor/outdoor feel to a finely dressed pool house by Thomas Pheasant.

OPPOSITE A custom hand-knotted rug suits the casual nature and colorful furnishings of a rustic cabin retreat decorated by John Peixinho.

ABOVE The reds and oranges of a custom hand-knotted patchwork rug extend the warm palette established by log walls and beams, together creating a snug atmosphere for an enclosed porch decorated by Juan Montoya.

ABOVE Joan Patryce dressed a playroom in complementary geometrics, with a carpet in the Berrow pattern providing a denser, thus harder-wearing, motif.

OPPOSITE In a playroom by Sheila Bridges, a Teo carpet from the Missoni Collection reads like a line drawing executed in crayon and acts to pull together the space's palette of primary colors.

ABOVE The tile-like Octagon carpet from the David Hicks Collection enlivens the neutral dress code of a billiard room tucked into a dormered space.

RIGHT On the floor of a sunny game room by Jan Showers, white dotted lines within the Antelope Ax pattern repeat the motif of spreading branches found both in the chandelier and in the landscape outside.

OPPOSITE In a formal Palm Beach billiard room by Michael Simon the Moiré carpet picks up both the warm wood tones and the gold accents.

ABOVE The black binding of a Torry sisal area rug lends it a crisp edge that elevates it to the level of other furnishings in a game room by Sherrill Canet.

PRECEDING PAGES A custom Axminster plaid carpet delivers a dose of British clubbiness to a screening room furnished with traditional upholstery by Trisha Reger.

LEFT A jazzy carpet in the Barnum pattern picks up the Deco tune established by red leather seating in a screening room by Linda Ruderman.

BELOW A custom hand-tufted silk carpet defines the viewing area in a game room by Mojo Stumer Associates.

RIGHT The brindled coloring and varied patterning of a cowhide rug lend a luxurious tortoiseshell effect to an otherwise monochromatic media room by Bill Bennette.

Mojo Stumer Associates enlisted a custom hand-tufted carpet with ripples of current from the Nina Campbell Collection to ensure that even when the yacht is still, the monochromatic seating area experiences movement.

ABOVE Beneath a yacht's lustrous coffered ceiling all is soft and natural, including the sisal carpet in a living area designed by Trisha Reger.

OVERLEAF Overscaled ropes and knots shaped by hand tufting and cutting create a gracefully abstract maritime motif for a custom carpet in the saloon of a yacht decorated by Geoffrey Bradfield.

BEDROOMS

THE BEDROOM IS THE PADDED NEST THAT launches us into the day and embraces us at day's end. It is the most personal place in the house because it is where our most private activities take place. No matter how streamlined the rest of the house may be, there are two things that no bedroom can be without if it is to make us feel rested and renewed: a mattress and a carpet.

A carpet is just as critical to a good night's sleep as a mattress. A lush envelope of protection, it muffles sound from other floors and from footsteps within the bedroom. It caresses us physically when we are at our most exposed. Of all the carpets in the house, it's the one that our bare feet are guaranteed to come in contact with.

Wall-to-wall carpeting may seem outré elsewhere in the house, but in bedrooms it has roared back into fashion. For good reason, says Jeffrey Bilhuber, who uses it exclusively in the bedrooms he decorates. "Nothing feels more cosseting. Its plushness and soundproofing allow you to sink into luxurious quietude."

Visually, a mattress is a mattress is a mattress. A carpet, on the other hand, is an element of beauty that visually sustains and magnifies comfort. No wonder, then, that its palette is often an extension of the other colors in the room and its hues are often soft and pale. It helps, of course, that the bedroom is usually the space furthest removed from outside dirt being tracked in.

The canopy bed on page 201 seems to emerge from the carpet on which it sits. A tight geometric rug supports the tailored bed hangings, its two tones referencing the banded canopy and bed curtains. In a more feminine version, the flourishes of a delicately colored antique Aubusson practically entwine with the gauzy tendrils cascading at the head of a gilded four-poster (page 200).

In bedrooms where richly colored furnishings take center stage, such as those on pages 220, 221, 224, and 225, pale carpets partner with walls similar in tone to provide a seamless neutral backdrop. Just as the light walls highlight the profiles of sconces, mirrors, and art, light carpets set off the rich grains and strong forms of wood furniture.

Charlotte Moss chose two layers of pale pattern for the carpets that furnish a large, elegant bedroom (pages 198–99). Her Shangri La pattern sisal rug lines the room while an Aubusson laid atop it defines a bed area that's distinct from the desk and lounge parts of the space. It's a layering technique she turns to often, especially when a room is so spacious.

A wallpaper's network of interlaced blossoming branches assumes a more rigorous geometry in Milan, a latticework-patterned Wilton carpet, run wall to wall in a bedroom suite by Guillaume Gentet.

"A smaller rug creates a room within a room," she says. "Having a sense of a more intimate space is particularly important in a bedroom. You want to demarcate work and rest areas. Plus, sisal is not usually the softest material, and I always want bare feet to have a cushiony place to land."

The ultimate sense of the bedroom as cocoon comes from a tone-on-tone treatment where the carpet is scarcely a different color but provides a shift in value via texture. Such is the case with John and Andrea Stark's bedroom in their Manhattan apartment (page 219). Designer Jeffrey Bilhuber created a glowing haven of a room in which the textiles are all solid colors in shades from café au lait to caramel. A silk wall-to-wall carpet brings luster and movement to the scheme. As it moves from bedroom to adjoining dressing room (page 218), it shifts not in hue but in pattern—quiet strié to more active geometric—reflecting the change in activity.

When pattern is in major play on bedroom walls, designers tend to take one of two tacks with floor coverings. They either select carpet that's an equal sparring partner or tone it down altogether to allow the wallpaper to shine. Scale and balance are the guiding lights more than pattern per se. A floral can partner with a geometric (page 211), as long as they are sympathetic in size of motif and coloration.

Guillaume Gentet chose a latticework design of carpet as the support for delicate blossoming branches on the wallpaper in the entry to a bedroom (page 193). The hues and medallions of the carpet in a guest bedroom by Alexa Hampton (page 209) are in such harmony with the formal wallpaper that they seem born of the same DNA. In a dormered bedroom by Charlotte Moss (left) a floral needlepoint rug atop floral tone-on-tone carpeting contributes more pattern to an already busy room, but the black ground of the rug brings a welcome weight to all the visual activity.

The stronger the wall pattern, the bolder the carpet can be, until the wallpaper utterly seizes the day. Then it's time for the carpet to step into a more subservient role. In bedrooms by Katie Ridder and Mario Buatta (pages 216, 217), the wallpaper is so saturated and lively that the carpets, though textured, provide a welcome visual rest.

A handmade needlepoint rug with many bouquets and a flowery border anchors the floral theme and contributes to the layering of pattern in a bedroom by Charlotte Moss.

RIGHT Peter Rogers accented his gray-paneled bedroom with art at eye level and a bold pattern, a brown-and-white Zebra cut-pile carpet, where it cannot distract from sleep.

OVERLEAF To establish a distinctly cozier island for the canopy bed in a grand bedroom, Charlotte Moss layered an antique Oushak carpet atop wall-to-wall sisal in the Shangri La pattern from her collection for Stark.

ABOVE In a bedroom by Solis Betancourt & Sherill, an antique Aubusson carpet reiterates the swags of curtains and canopy and the flowers in an antique textile hung at the head of the bed.

OPPOSITE David Hicks's Wye carpet in two shades of gray establishes a tailored base for a handsome bedroom by Steven Gambrel.

A custom hand-tufted carpet in
an exploded Prince of Wales pattern
littered with oversized flowers
holds its own against the strong
persimmon wall color of a niche
in this bedroom.

FLORAL AND CLASSIC

Floral and classic are nearly one and the same at Stark, as some of the earliest carpets the company produced were designs festooned with garlands, vines, bouquets, ribbons, and cartouches. Many of the patterns were derived from museum documents of Aubusson and Savonnerie rugs from the seventeenth century.

Stark was first to import to the United States petit- and gros-point rugs from France and needlework rugs from Portugal and Greece. The Montreaux carpet carries on the spirit of those traditional rugs. Its design, a dense pattern of sprigs of leaves and berries evenly scattered across a solid field, has never gone out of fashion. Pale ground colors of pistachio and seafoam suit bedrooms, while deeper tones of cognac and noir lay down a rich and practical base for studies and family rooms.

What worked centuries ago—graceful designs and soft palettes—still slips seamlessly into traditional interiors today. The Ravello pattern has been in the line for years. Its delicate flowers and light green vines twirling across a creamy ground turn any bedroom into a garden idyll. When floral patterns are rendered in a subtle tone-on-tone coloration, the effect is that of a rich brocade underfoot, delivering a sense of total luxury.

LEFT For all of its innovation and trendsetting, Stark has never forsaken pretty florals and handsome classic patterns that are a mainstay of traditional interiors. Clockwise from top: Montreaux Wide Noir, Floral Stria Blue, Ironwork Arizona, Needlepoint, Japanese Bouquet, a custom Tibetan.

RIGHT Machine woven in Europe to simulate period needlepoint rugs, "Petit Point" carpets from À La Place Clichy in Paris were one of first collections Stark imported to America.

•STARK CARPET CORP.
presents the
"Petit Point Group"*

"Transition"
Copy of Petit Point
Mid 18th Century

"Calla Lilies"
Copy of Antique Needlework

"Veronique"
Copy of English Petit Point

"Bessarabian"
Copy of Petit Point
Early 19th Century

The green Flambé linen carpet
in a bedroom by Markham Roberts
seems like an abstracted leafy trellis
from which vines have broken
away to climb the walls.

ABOVE A subtly ridged carpet, Ebbe & Flow, in a blend of wool, viscose, and cotton, picks up the blue of the wallpaper and the stripe of the dado in a girl's bedroom by McGeehan Design.

OPPOSITE Carpet in the Blakeville pattern maintains formality while moving the color scheme of russet and gold a notch lighter in a guest room by Alexa Hampton.

ABOVE A wool carpet in the Erica pattern captures in its fine net bolder motifs in the same blue-and-white color scheme that Cullman & Kravis devised for this master bedroom.

RIGHT The overscaled caning pattern of Howard Slatkin's Basketweave carpet for Stark provides a geometric regularity to ground a guest room of his design that exuberantly embraces a crisp and vivacious floral.

OPPOSITE Vittoria, a striped carpet from the Missoni Collection, is an energetic yet practical choice for a guest bedroom in a Montana house decorated by Juan Montoya.

ABOVE The warm colors and chevron pattern of a thick, custom flatweave carpet give a bedroom in Montana the appeal and comfort of a luxurious multi-ply sweater.

LEFT Designer David Scott's choice of a patchwork rug, composed of striped and checked pieces of kilim carpets, maintains an atmosphere of elevated rusticity in a bedroom dominated by a fieldstone fireplace.

ABOVE A wall-to-wall carpet woven of jute matches the tone but counters the weight of rustic beams in a lodge bedroom decorated by Markham Roberts.

The Feast of Love

THE GARDEN PLANNER · WILLIAMS

A Handful of Flowers

THE ELEMENTS OF ORGANIC GARDENING · HRH THE PRINCE OF WALES

MARY McDONALD INTERIORS

OPPOSITE A Clay Stria wool carpet in pecan from the Alexa Hampton
Collection adds geometric tone-on-tone pattern that doesn't compete with
the exaggerated florals of the wallpaper in a bedroom by Katie Ridder.

ABOVE Wall-to-wall Saranac sisal deliberately plays second fiddle to the mix of
curvaceous furnishings and floral wallcovering in a bedroom by Mario Buatta.

ABOVE Carpet in the Callaway pattern picks up on the geometric rhythm created by drawer pulls and nailheads in the dressing room that Jeffrey Bilhuber designed for Andrea Stark.

OPPOSITE Jeffrey Bilhuber chose a subtly strié carpet, Ebbe & Flow in taupe, to provide cocooning underfoot and match the cosseting of upholstered walls in Andrea and John Stark's bedroom.

ABOVE Carpet in the Milden Hall pattern and scenic wallpaper in similar pale tones provide a quiet backdrop for the strong form of a handsome combination bench and chest in a bedroom by Redmond Aldrich Design.

RIGHT Massucco Warner Miller chose a custom carpet in a shade nearly indistinguishable from that of the walls to create a seamless light envelope for furnishings in rich dark colors.

ABOVE In a bedroom loaded with flavor in the colors and patterns of wallpaper, curtains, headboard, lamp, and pillows, Katie Ridder chose plain vanilla as a "palette" cleanser for the bound carpet.

OPPOSITE In Ashley Stark Kenner's dressing room by James Aman and John Meeks, a wall-to-wall Samora carpet establishes a neutral platform for an antique desk, while a round fox-fur rug links flashier pieces like a Lucite chair and mirrored dresser.

OPPOSITE The white trellislike pattern of a custom Wilton carpet in a bedroom by Thomas Pheasant connects to the French doors and balcony railing beyond, further opening up an already airy space.

ABOVE Sometimes the plainest carpet of all, such as this custom Tibetan, can be the most quiet and restful, especially when paired with other solids as in this bedroom by Carrier and Company.

OVERLEAF The sitting area and bed float on a plane of custom ivory-colored carpet in a bedroom by April Powers that itself hovers above vineyards in California wine country.

OPPOSITE In a bedroom by Trudy Dujardin, the carpet in the Dante pattern of interlocking squares from the Alexa Hampton Collection contrasts with unadorned rust-colored walls and connects with the Greek key handles of a bedside dresser.

ABOVE The overall pitter-patter motif of a Cheetah Cub carpet in honey tones balances the weight of an upholstered wall in deepest plum in a bedroom by Iain Halliday.

OVERLEAF Howard Slatkin's diamond-patterned Rex carpet slips readily into a mix of marquetry dressers, herringbone headboard, and houndstooth-weave blanket in a bedroom he designed.

SMALL CASTLES AND PAVILIONS OF EUROPE

FRANÇOISE GILOT
Monograph   1940-2000

OPPOSITE A field of mottled indigo provided by a custom flatweave carpet bridges the denim color of the walls and the pure white of the window shades and bed linens in a bedroom by Lindsey Coral Harper.

ABOVE In a bedroom by Eric Cohler, floor-to-ceiling wooden blinds provide one modern geometry, wool carpet in David Hicks's Logo pattern another—both the better to offset antique and modern furniture chosen for form.

OPPOSITE A crisp blue-and-white Catania carpet extends the nautical theme of a seaside bedroom decorated by Interiors by BLP.

TOP A bedroom created by Amy Thebault for a Yankees fan features pinstripes for the walls and a field of blue littered with confetti in the custom rug for the floor.

ABOVE Triangle Interiors used Antelope Ax carpet to pull together multiple references to animals in this bedroom.

ABOVE Disks of the looped-wool Argento carpet pad the floor of a snug desk area that Finchatton tucked into a house in London.

OPPOSITE The black-and-white Beaton geometric carpet from the Diamond Baratta Collection brings practical pizzazz to a girl's bedroom created by Amanda Nisbet.

THE
STARK
TRADITION

SOMETIMES, WHEN COMPANIES grow large and become leaders in their field, it's hard to remember that they started with nothing more than an instinct. Such is the case with Stark Carpet. Arthur Stark, a businessman at heart and by training, also had a prescient feel for the design world and what might excite it.

At first his knowledge of carpets was scant, picked up from relatives who were in the carpet distribution business and from sharing an office for a time with Edward Fields, another early innovator in the industry. But on trips to Europe, Stark indulged his passion for antiques and trained his eye to identify special things, primarily carpets that were unavailable back in the United States.

Stark became the first to import luxurious European handmade and machine-made patterned carpets to the U.S., a pioneering and risky move made all the more remarkable given its timing. From founding the company with his wife, Nadia, in 1938 to incorporating it in New York in 1946, Stark grew a business rooted in trips to Europe in the midst of World War II.

If there was one thing that characterized Arthur Stark, it was a restless curiosity that led to innovation. His legacy of uniting the handmade with the technological and thereby introducing something different, indeed sometimes revolutionary, to the design world remains the company's guiding principle and driving force.

Broadloom is such a common carpet term that we take for granted the ready availability of carpets in wide widths. But prior to 1950, the industry standard

Ashley Stark Kenner has updated the Stark palette to include many more grays, such as that of the Spellbind pattern, a variation on the Moiré pattern.

Rainbow X

Velvet Broadloom

Electra Blue	Beige	Emerald Green	Stone
Putty	Cardinal Red	Pastel Green	Charcoal
Tete De Negre	White	Moss Green	Gold
Cerise	Aqua	Wheat	Blue
Sauterne	Bronze	Grey	Hunter Green

Rainbox X, an unprecedented collection of plush wool velvet carpet in twenty rich colors and extra-wide widths, upended the world of design in 1950.

for carpet looms was 27 inches. A room-size carpet was composed of numerous strips painstakingly stitched together by skilled installers, which only added to the sense of carpet as a luxury item.

Perhaps Arthur Stark's greatest contribution to the design world was the introduction of high-quality, 100 percent wool velvet carpets in widths of 12, 15, and 18 feet. Working with a loom manufacturer in Germany, he developed new equipment in 1950 that produced these broad carpets in an unprecedented array of colors. A factory that had pumped out uniforms during the war was happy to be busy once again and to be in the business of bringing a little softness to a bruised world.

The plush wall-to-wall carpet that paved many a high-end postwar interior came from Stark's Rainbow X collection. The plain velvet weave, available in twenty rich colors, became a new hallmark of luxury, a startling expanse of color that delighted the eye and caressed the feet. In the lingering gloomy palette of postwar America, Stark's innovation set the design world alight.

Many of the detailed patterned carpets that Stark produced were adaptations of museum documents. For those who fancied the look of an antique Aubusson or Savonnerie rug but preferred the durability of a new carpet, not to mention a custom size, Stark provided reproductions. Made in France, they were true in design and weave to seventeenth-century originals. French custom Point de Lys rugs in a plush velour texture and French linen rugs as fine and soft as antique silk rugs followed. In 1957

Stark brought Petit Point carpets from Paris's carpet emporium À La Place Clichy to America. The mechanically woven rugs faithfully reproduced the look of handmade needlework designs featuring trellises, flowers, and combinations of the two.

Designers and decorators are always on the prowl for a great new resource. To find rugs in such elegant patterns, customizable in size, color, and format—with or without border—was to hit the decorating jackpot. In 1961 none other than Stéphane Boudin of Maison Jansen, the decorating firm Jacqueline Kennedy stealthily employed to bring sophistication to the White House, came calling.

Stark's work for the Kennedy

Stark has always been known for faithful reproductions of historic rugs such as these Petit Point carpets from France, which the company introduced to the U.S. in the late 1950s.

administration was the beginning of a long relationship with presidential interiors. The company supplied everything from the Snowflake pattern carpet that Boudin specified for the China Room (where the state china is displayed) to the Empire Caissons carpet in the Nixon family's private dining room to the eagle-crested carpet in Reagan's Oval Office.

Stark has always been adept at detecting trends and modifying carpets to suit. Arthur Stark came across traditional Portuguese and Greek needlepoint rugs and cast them in more contemporary colors. He did the same with traditional kilims and dhurries. He put punch into traditional plaids and introduced animal patterns that made decorators like Billy Baldwin swoon. Nadia Stark, originally a milliner, had the notion to combine floral and animal motifs, resulting in the iconic Leopard Rose pattern, whose popularity has never waned. Their son Steven Stark took a

LEFT AND BELOW Ronald Reagan's
Oval Office carpet, shown underway
in a Stark workroom and in situ on
Reagan's last day in office, featured
sunbeams radiating from a central
presidential seal.

OPPOSITE Arthur Stark drew great
inspiration from Owen Jones's *Grammar
of Ornament*, originally published in 1856.
The Hadera, Large Hexagon, and Wye
patterns trace their roots to a page
of Chinese motifs.

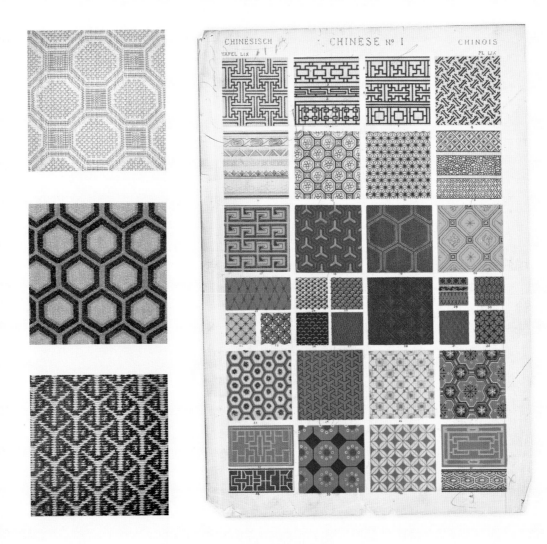

photograph of the carpet in the lobby of the Negresco hotel in Nice, and soon Stark was offering a Wilton carpet named Negresco.

Though geometric carpets are associated almost exclusively with legendary British decorator David Hicks, he and Arthur Stark discovered them virtually simultaneously in the late 1960s. When Hicks questioned Stark about poaching his designs, Stark pointed to the exact page in a hundred-year-old tome, Owen Jones's *Grammar of Ornament*, that both had turned to for inspiration. Today Stark carries the Hicks Collection alongside its own geometrics.

Arthur Stark's premature passing in 1968 pitched his sons, John and Steven, into the business straight from college. Aided by their mother for a decade, they carried on the family tradition of nurturing relationships with designers, adopting innovative techniques, including the conversion of looms to produce 12-foot-wide patterned carpets, and introducing an array of different and exclusive carpets.

The third generation, cousins Ashley Stark Kenner and Chad Stark, is now ascendant at Stark.

The brothers grew Stark from two showrooms to more than twenty and, with the acquisition of Grey Watkins, Fonthill Fabrics, and Old World Weavers, extended the company's design reach into fabric and wallpaper. To accommodate our time's co-obsession with luxury and I-want-it-now, they have an American mill that can turn out a Wilton carpet in half the standard time and stock more than a hundred high-end machine-made carpet lines, as well as thirty to forty handmade lines in broadloom and thousands of hand-knotted rugs. Many of these carpets can take artisans in India and China nine months to make by hand.

Like their fathers, cousins Ashley Stark Kenner and Chad Stark have joined the family business. Their youthful outlook has already brought changes to the company in the form of a redesign of the original Manhattan showroom in the Decoration & Design Building, an updated palette reflecting contemporary taste, and a website that engages and informs everyone interested in fine design.

Ashley and Chad are dedicated not just to maintaining Stark as the leader it has always been but also to advancing its interests in the twin pillars of design and technology on which it has always stood. As it was, so shall it continue—a Stark carpet knows no bounds. If you can dream it up, they can weave it.

Carabello carpet introduces welcome pattern, along with luscious color, to a library by Penny Drue Baird that is dominated by solids.

ACKNOWLEDGMENTS

First and foremost, we would like to thank the design community—the designers featured in this book and the thousands of others who have supported Stark for more than seventy-five years. Their commitment to our products has made us the success that we are today. We are grateful to the Stark community, the countless hard-working artisans—from those in our fabrication headquarters in Calhoun, Georgia, to those in our mills all over the world—as well as the hundreds of dedicated team members in our more than twenty showrooms worldwide. We are also deeply appreciative of the design press—the many editors, writers, and bloggers—who have championed us.

We would like to thank the many people who have contributed to this book: Heather Smith MacIsaac, who helped to crystallize our thoughts into words; the world-class photographers whose work illustrates these pages; our agent, Karen Gantz, who worked tirelessly on our behalf; and the editorial, design, and production team at Vendome, without whom this book could not have been produced.

Finally, we would like to thank our fathers, John and Steven Stark, and our grandparents Arthur and Nadia Stark, who instilled in us a love of design and the design industry, which will carry Stark forward for future generations. We also extend heartfelt gratitude to each of our mothers, Andrea Stark and Candice Stark, for the values and ethics that they instilled in us; these qualities drive everything that we do.

Ashley Stark Kenner and Chad Stark

▪ ▪ ▪

INDEX OF DESIGNERS

Mojo Stumer: pp. 135, 186 bottom, 188

Juan Montoya: pp. 177, 212, 213

Charlotte Moss: pp. 6, 11 top, 34, 113, 116, 194–95, 198–99, 211

Munger Interiors: p. 97

Amanda Nesbit: p. 237

Carl Palasota: back cover, p. 19

Alex Papachristidis: pp. 10 bottom left, 139

Joan Patryce/J. Patryce Designs: p. 178

John Peixinho: p. 176

Thomas Pheasant: pp. 8, 174–75, 224

April Powers: pp. 226–7

Trisha Reger: pp. 60, 121, 153, 156, 184–85, 189

Suzanne Rheinstein: pp. 46–47

Katie Ridder: p. 142–43, 216, 222

Markham Roberts: pp. 54–55, 101, 132, 206–7, 215

Peter Rogers: pp. 196–97

Linda Ruderman: pp. 53, 186 top

Kelter Schwartz: p. 86

David Scott Interiors: p. 214–15

Steven Shadley: p. 57

Sherrill Canet Interiors: pp. 82, 183

Bruce Shostak: p. 66

Jan Showers: pp. 106, 108, 125, 180–181

Marjorie Shushan: pp. 22–23

Michael Simon: pp. 52–53, 182

Howard Slatkin: front cover, pp. 2–3, 110–11, 230–31

Michael Smith: p. 56

Solis Betancourt & Sherrill: pp. 27, 200

Amy Thebault: pp. 26, 30, 98–99, 235 top

Triangle Interiors: pp. 95, 235 bottom

Amy Vermillion: p. 162

Ashley Whittaker: p. 144

Bunny Williams: pp. 118–19

Tod Williams and Billie Tsien Architects: pp. 78, 79

Bebe Winkler: p. 73

Witmer Design: p. 61

Vicente Wolf: p. 131

Scot Meacham Wood: p. 126

■ ■ ■

PHOTO CREDITS

Michel Arnaud: p. 183

Mali Azima: pp. 10 bottom right, 140–41, 167

Jim Bartsch: pp. 28–29

Gordon Beall: pp. 220–21

Philip Beaurline: p. 27

Antoine Bootz: pp. 214, 228

Andrew Bordwin: p. 94

Brantley Photography: pp. 32, 90, 91, 122–23, 158–59, 190–91

Scott Chebegia: pp. 226–27

Pascal Chevallier/ thelicensingproject.com: pp. 92–93, 219

Patrick Cline: p. 109

Paul Costello/OTTO: p. 77

© Tom Crane: p. 70, 152

Grey Crawford: pp. 154–55

Photos originally published in *Architectural Digest*. Roger Davies, photographer: pp. 31, 74–75, 102–3

Erica George Dines: p. 35

Chris Edwards: p. 162

Phillip Ennis: pp. 1, 60, 80–81, 153, 184–85, 189

Pieter Estersohn: pp. 6–8, 10 top right, 11 top, 20–21, 45, 113, 116, 179, 194–95, 211, 237; photos originally published in *Architectural Digest*: pp. 46–47, 131

Scott Frances/OTTO: pp. 22–23, 209; photos originally published in *Architectural Digest*: pp. 24,

57, 58–59, 117, 180–81, 217

Steve Freihon: pp. 96, 136–37

Douglas Friedman/Trunk Archive: front cover, pp. 2–3, 107, 110–11, 230–31

Morris Gindi Photography: p. 33

Tria Giovan: pp. 10 bottom left, 139, 202–3

Tom Grimes: p. 83

Dirck Halstead/Hulton Archive/ Getty Images: pp. 242

Cristi Harvey Photography (Houston, TX): p. 235 bottom

Philip Harvey/© 2012 philipharvey.com: p. 126

Edward Hill Photography: pp. 186–87

Michael Hunter: p. 97

Thibault Jeanson: pp. 168, 169

Gwynn Johnson: p. 53

Nick Johnson: p. 82

Ben Johnston: pp. 68–69, 134

Laure Joliet: p. 220

Stephen Karlisch: p. 106

Nathan Kirkman: p. 216

Nikolas Koenig/OTTO. Photos originally published in *Architectural Digest*: pp. 4–5, 76, 78, 79

Francesco Lagnese: p. 37

Jan La Salle: p. 73

© Chris Little Photography, Atlanta, GA: p. 149

Thomas Loof: pp. 101, 176

Lucas Studio Inc./Karyn R. Millet: p. 41

Lee Manning / leemanningphoto.com: pp. 114–15

Jeff McNamara: p. 108, 125

Mark Menjivar: p. 100

Matthew Millman: pp. 36–37

Moris Moreno: p. 164–65

Charlotte Moss: p. 34 right

Ngoc Minh Ngo: p. 232

Tim Peters/timpetersphoto.com: pp. 30, 98–99

Eric Piasecki/OTTO: pp. 10 top left, 14, 14–15, 17, 40, 50–51, 88–89, 104, 121, 124, 142–43, 144, 148, 150–51, 163, 177, 201, 210, 212, 213, 222, 223, 225; photos originally published in *Architectural Digest*: back cover, pp. 19, 120, 145, 156, 196–97

Dan Piassick: pp. 95, 234

Marco Ricca: pp. 54–55, 127, 206–7

Mark Roskams: pp. 11 bottom, 193

Lisa Ross: p. 178

Eric Roth: pp. 26, 42, 43, 170–71

Hector M. Sanchez: pp. 84–85, 157

© Kim Sargent: p. 172–73

Durston Saylor Photography: pp. 8, 174–75, 224, 244

Annie Schlechter: p. 208

James Schriebl: p. 235 top

Beth Singer: pp. 61, 72, 86

Walter Smalling Jr.: p. 200

Julie Soefer: p. 87

Tim Street-Porter: p. 105

Eric Striffler: pp. 34 left, 198–99

Mark Stumer: pp. 186 bottom, 188

Christopher Sturman/Trunk Archive: p. 120

Tom Sullam: p. 236

Senen Ubiña/UV Studios Photography: pp. 160, 161, 218

Simon Upton: pp. 67, 182

Jason Varney: p. 180

Peter Vitale: p. 71

Fritz von der Schulenburg: pp. 118–19

Yale Wagner: p. 233

William Waldron: pp. 18, 25, 48–49, 64–65, 66, 229

Björn Wallander/OTTO. Photos originally published in *Architectural Digest*: pp. 56, 130, 132, 133, 215

Paul Warchol: p. 135

Best efforts were made to verify all photo credits. Any oversight was unintentional, and should be brought to the publisher's attention so that it can be corrected in a future printing.

First published in the United States of America by
The Vendome Press
1334 York Avenue
New York, NY 10021
www.vendomepress.com

ISBN 978-0-86565-322-1

EDITOR: Jacqueline Decter
PRODUCTION COORDINATOR: Jim Spivey
DESIGNER: Celia Fuller

Library of Congress Cataloging-in-Publication Data

Kenner, Ashley Stark, author.
Decorating with carpets : a fine foundation / Ashley Stark Kenner and
Chad Stark ; with Heather Smith MacIsaac.
    pages cm
  ISBN 978-0-86565-322-1 (hardback)
1. Rugs in interior decoration. I. Stark, Chad, author. II. MacIsaac,
Heather Smith. III. Title.
NK2115.5.R77K46 2015
747'.5–dc23
                                                    2015028005

This book was produced using acid-free paper, processed
chlorine free, and printed with soy-based inks.

PRINTED IN CHINA BY OGI
FIRST PRINTING

PAGE 1 A living room by Thomas Jayne features a starburst carpet from his
collection for Stark Carpet (see also pages 80–81).

PAGES 2–3 Liliane carpet lays a chic foundation for other fine furnishings in a
living room by Howard Slatkin (see pages 110–11 for another view of the same room).

PAGES 4–5 Twin hand-stitched cowhide rugs define separate but equal seating
areas in Donny Deutsch's living room designed by Tony Ingrao and Randy
Kemper (see also page 76).

PAGES 6–7 Charlotte Moss chose a sisal carpet to lighten the formality of her
traditionally decorated living room in the Hamptons.

PAGE 8 The texture of a custom carpet plays off the rattan seats and backs of
the chairs in a dining room by Thomas Pheasant.

PAGES 9–10, TOP ROW, LEFT TO RIGHT stair hall by Steven Gambrel
(see page 17), living room by Thomas Jayne (see page 45), study by Charlotte
Moss (see page 113); BOTTOM ROW, LEFT TO RIGHT dining room by Alex
Papachristidis (see page 139), playroom by Margaret Kirkland (see page 167),
bedroom by Guillaume Gentet (see page 193).